from SEA TO SHINING SEA

INDIANA

By Dennis Brindell Fradin and Judith Bloom Fradin

CONSULTANTS

Ralph D. Gray, Ph.D., Professor of History, Indiana University at Indianapolis;
Editor, *Journal of the Early Republic*

Robert L. Hillerich, Ph.D., Professor Emeritus, Bowling Green State University;
Consultant, Pinellas County Schools, Florida

CHILDRENS PRESS®

CHICAGO

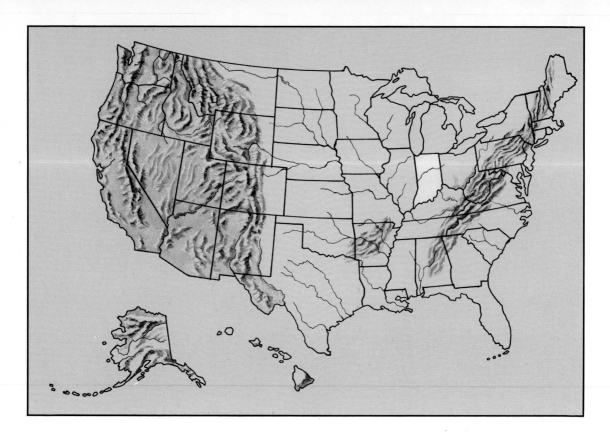

Indiana is one of the twelve states in the region called the Midwest. The other Midwest states are Illinois, Iowa, Kansas, Michigan, Minnesota, Missouri, Nebraska, North Dakota, Ohio, South Dakota, and Wisconsin.

For our Aunt Elaine Cohen, with love

Front cover picture: State capitol, Indianapolis; page 1: Lighthouse, Michigan City; back cover: Redbud tree and covered bridge, Cataract Falls State Park

Project Editor: Joan Downing
Design Director: Karen Kohn
Typesetting: Graphic Connections, Inc.
Engraving: Liberty Photoengraving

Library of Congress Cataloging-in-Publication Data

Fradin, Dennis B.
  Indiana / by Dennis Brindell Fradin & Judith Bloom
Fradin.
    p.   cm. — (From sea to shining sea)
  Includes index.
  ISBN 0-516-03814-1
  1. Indiana—Juvenile literature. I. Fradin, Judith Bloom.
II. Title. III. Series: Fradin, Dennis B. From sea to
shining sea.
F526.3.F69   1994   94-6234
977.2—dc20   CIP
                                                             AC

Table of Contents

Introducing the Hoosier State 4

"On the Banks of the Wabash, Far Away". 7

From Ancient Times Until Today 13

Hoosiers and Their Work. 29

A Hoosier State Tour 32

A Gallery of Famous Hoosiers 47

Did You Know? 54

Indiana Information 56

Indiana History. 58

Map of Indiana 60

Glossary 61

Index. 63

Irish Guard in formation at a Notre Dame football game

Introducing the Hoosier State

*I*ndiana is a state in the Midwest. Long ago, many Indian tribes lived in the area. The state's name means "land of the Indians." Indiana's nickname is the "Hoosier State." Indiana people are called Hoosiers. Many stories are told about this nickname's origin.

During the Revolutionary War, the Americans gained key posts in Indiana. This helped the United States claim the area after the war. Pioneers quickly settled the land. They farmed and built cities and factories. Three presidents of the United States had homes in Indiana.

Today, Indiana leads the country at making steel. It is also a leader at growing corn and soybeans. The state is a leader at mining coal, too. Indiana also has produced many talented authors.

The Hoosier State is famous in other ways. Where are Purdue and Notre Dame universities found? Where is the Indianapolis 500 auto race held? Where is the town of Santa Claus? Where were basketball-great Larry Bird and dancer Twyla Tharp born? What state is first at growing corn for popping? The answer to these questions is: Indiana!

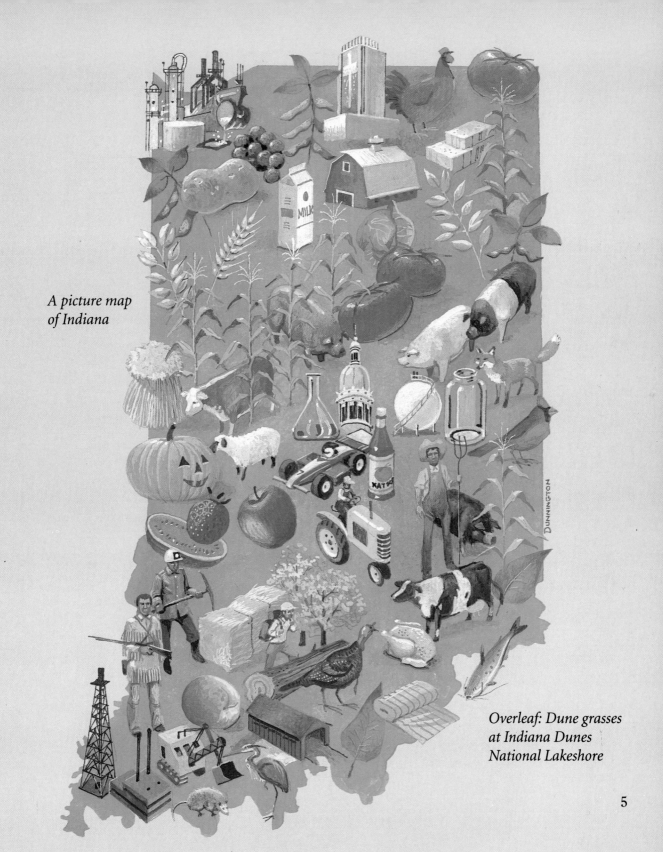

A picture map
of Indiana

*Overleaf: Dune grasses
at Indiana Dunes
National Lakeshore*

5

"On the Banks of the Wabash, Far Away"

"On the Banks of the Wabash, Far Away"

Indiana covers 36,291 square miles. It is the smallest of the midwestern states. Indiana is also one of the Great Lakes states. Lake Michigan, one of the five Great Lakes, touches northwest Indiana. Four states border Indiana. Michigan is to the north. Ohio lies to the east. Kentucky is to the south and southeast. Illinois is to the west.

Wetlands and woods in autumn, Indiana Dunes State Park

South-central Indiana is hilly. Many caves lie in those hills. Much oil and coal are also found there. The rest of the state is rather level. Rich soil makes northern and central Indiana great for farming.

Lakes and Rivers

Northwest Indiana has 40 miles of Lake Michigan shoreline. Lake Michigan is the largest lake completely inside the United States. There are more than 400 much smaller lakes within Indiana. Most are natural lakes, such as Lake Wawasee. Some are man-made lakes, such as Lake Monroe.

The Wabash is Indiana's longest river. The Wabash begins in Ohio. But most of its 475-mile journey is within Indiana. The Wabash continues

TOPOGRAPHY

Below Sea Level	100 m. 328 ft.	200 m. 656 ft.	500 m. 1,640 ft.	1,000 m. 3,281 ft.	2,000 m. 6,562 ft.	5,000 m. 16,404 ft.

along Indiana's western border. The White, Tippecanoe, and Kankakee are among Indiana's other rivers. The Ohio River forms Indiana's southern border.

Left: Prickly-pear cactuses and wild roses

WOODS AND WILDLIFE

One-sixth of the state is wooded. The tulip tree is the state tree. Dogwoods, redbuds, sycamores, maples, oaks, and pines also grow in Indiana.

Prickly-pear cactuses grow in sandy areas. Jack-in-the-pulpits and violets are other Indiana plants.

Deer and foxes roam Indiana's woods. Beavers, raccoons, and opossums live in Indiana, too. The cardinal is the state bird. Bluebirds, sparrows, robins, and woodpeckers also fly about. Bass, catfish, and sunfish swim Indiana's waters.

CLIMATE

Indiana has warm summers and cool winters. Summer temperatures average about 80 degrees

Bluebird

Left: Skunk cabbage at Cowles Bog
Right: Wild rye and grasses in autumn

Fahrenheit. Temperatures around 30 degrees Fahrenheit are common in winter. Northern Indiana receives about 5 feet of snow each winter. Southern Indiana gets only about 1 foot.

Melting snow and spring rains often cause flooding on Indiana's rivers. Several tornadoes twist across Indiana each year.

Cataract Falls, Cataract Falls State Park

11

FROM ANCIENT TIMES UNTIL TODAY

About 2 million years ago, the Ice Age began. During this cold period, most of Indiana was blanketed by glaciers. These moving ice masses flattened the land. Southern Indiana is hilly because glaciers did not reach that area. Mammoths and mastodons roamed Indiana during the Ice Age. These animals were ancestors of today's elephants.

Opposite: A fife and drum corps at the Feast of the Hunter's Moon, West Lafayette

AMERICAN INDIANS

The first Indianans were prehistoric Indians. They reached Indiana more than 10,000 years ago. The Ice Age was ending as they arrived. Their ancient spear points have been unearthed.

More than 2,000 years ago, the Indians started building huge dirt mounds. Many were burial places. Others were forts or religious centers. The mound-building Indians left behind pottery, jewelry, and stone carvings.

During the 1700s, more Indians moved to Indiana. The Miamis made up one of the biggest tribes in Indiana. They lived in wigwams made of

A reconstructed stockade at Angel Mounds State Park

bark and animal skins. The Miamis grew corn and squash at their villages. They also hunted deer and bears with bows and arrows. Other tribes in Indiana included the Delaware, Shawnee, and Kickapoo.

FRENCH AND ENGLISH RULE

The French were the first Europeans in Indiana. French explorer René-Robert Cavelier, Sieur de La Salle, arrived in 1679. He reached what is now the city of South Bend. In 1681, he met with Miami Indians under the Council Oak. This huge tree was a South Bend landmark until it fell in 1991.

France claimed much of North America, including Indiana. Starting in the early 1700s, French fur traders traveled through Indiana. They exchanged blankets and beads for the Indians' beaver furs. The French built trading posts and forts in Indiana. One fort built in 1732 grew into Vincennes. Another became Lafayette.

The beaver furs were made into hats and coats.

French priests and farmers joined the fur traders and soldiers. But France's hold on Indiana was weak. By 1750, only 100 French settlers were in the region.

During those same years, England had founded thirteen colonies. They were along the Atlantic

A frontiersman fixing dinner at the Chellberg Farm, Indiana Dunes National Lakeshore

Ocean. In 1754, England and France went to war. This was called the French and Indian War (1754-1763). England won the war. French land including Indiana then passed to English rule. But only a few British fur traders and soldiers went there.

Indians helped the French, and colonists fought on the side of the English in the French and Indian War.

GEORGE ROGERS CLARK AND THE REVOLUTIONARY WAR

The French and Indian War had cost England much money. To make up those costs, England placed more taxes on the colonists. The Americans would not pay them. In 1775, the thirteen colonies rebelled against England. They began fighting the

George Rogers Clark

Little Turtle

Revolutionary War (1775-1783). The Americans set up a new country. They called it the United States of America.

The war was mainly fought in the East. But in 1778-79, Virginian George Rogers Clark led about 180 men west. They marched into present-day Illinois and Indiana. Clark's men captured two British outposts in Illinois. They also captured the fort at Vincennes, Indiana. Clark's victories helped America's claims to these lands.

THE TERRITORIAL YEARS

As a result of the Revolutionary War, the United States doubled in size. England gave up all its land east of the Mississippi River. In 1787, the United States Congress passed the Northwest Ordinance. This law created the Northwest Territory, which included Indiana. It also outlawed slavery in the territory.

By 1788, about 20,000 Americans had moved to the Northwest Territory. Most of them lived in Ohio. The Indians there feared that they would lose their lands. Miami chief Little Turtle formed a large army. Little Turtle's army won battles against United States soldiers. But in 1794, General "Mad Anthony" Wayne crushed the Indians. That battle took place in what is now Ohio. Little Turtle and other chiefs then made peace. Wayne went on to Indiana and built Fort Wayne.

In 1800, the Indiana Territory was created. About 5,000 people lived there. The territory included present-day Indiana, Illinois, Michigan and Wisconsin. William Henry Harrison was named governor of the territory. Vincennes was the capital. By 1809, the Indiana Territory contained only present-day Indiana.

During those years, two Shawnee brothers were rising to power. Tecumseh was a warrior. Tenskwatawa was a religious leader. The brothers brought members of many tribes together. They

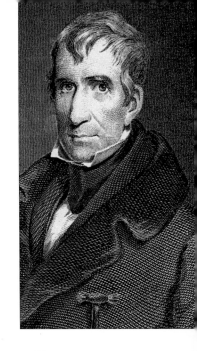

William Henry Harrison

The North Blockhouse, at Historic Fort Wayne

Harrison's campaign slogan was "Tippecanoe and Tyler Too." John Tyler was Harrison's vice president. Harrison died after only one month in office.

The Battle of Tippecanoe

decided to defend their lands against the settlers. But in 1811, Governor Harrison's forces defeated the Indians. This battle took place in northwest Indiana. It is called the Battle of Tippecanoe. Harrison became a hero. He was known as "Tippecanoe." That name was part of his campaign slogan in 1840. In 1841, he became the ninth president of the United States.

Meanwhile, pioneer families were pouring into Indiana. They built log cabins and began new towns. The Lincolns, from Kentucky, were one of those families. In 1816, Abraham Lincoln's family moved to southern Indiana. Lincoln helped his father build the family cabin and plant crops. For a

short time, he attended a backwoods school. The family left Indiana in 1830 and settled in Illinois.

The first state capitol, in Corydon

THE NINETEENTH STATE

By 1815, Indiana had 64,000 people. That was more than enough to become a state. On December 11, 1816, the United States Congress made Indiana the nineteenth state. Corydon was Indiana's first state capital. It was in far southeastern Indiana.

In 1820, Indiana lawmakers made plans for a new capital. Indianapolis was then built in the middle of the state. Its name means "City of Indiana." Indianapolis has been the state capital since 1825.

Indiana's state flag has nineteen stars because Indiana was the nineteenth state to join the Union.

The old Opera House,
New Harmony

A state's constitution
contains its basic laws.

Indiana became known as the Hoosier State. Some say the word *Hoosier* came from an old word meaning "hill." Others say the name is from Sam Hoosier. He hired Indianans for his Kentucky work crews. The Indianans were called Hoosier's men. According to another story, Indianans greeted new pioneers with the words "Who's here?" They said it so fast that it sounded like "Hoosier."

Education has long been important in Indiana. Indiana's constitution of 1816 provided for free public schools. It was the first state constitution to do that. The schools were to be "open to all."

In 1814, George Rapp founded the town of New Harmony. Robert Owen bought the town from Rapp in 1825. Many teachers came to New Harmony. They set up one of the world's first nursery schools. They also had one of the country's first coeducational schools. Those are schools in which boys and girls study together. New Harmony's schools helped shape American education.

THE CIVIL WAR

Indiana was a free state. Slavery had been outlawed there since 1787. However, slavery was allowed in southern states. Many Indiana pioneers came from the South. They brought their slaves with them. Finally, in 1843, Indianans no longer held slaves.

Meanwhile, thousands of southern slaves were fleeing to freedom in Canada. Many Hoosiers helped them on their journey. Levi and Katie Coffin lived in Fountain City. They hid more than 2,000 slaves from 1826 to 1847. A southern slave-hunter noted how escaped slaves disappeared in Indiana. "They must have an underground railroad here," he said. "And Levi Coffin must be its president." The network that helped slaves escape was called the Underground Railroad.

A spinning wheel at New Harmony

This Civil War soldier was from Fulton County.

In 1860, Abraham Lincoln was elected the sixteenth president of the United States. After that, eleven southern states left the Union. They feared that Lincoln would try to end slavery. Between 1861 and 1865, the northern and southern states fought the Civil War. Slavery was a cause of the war.

The only fighting in Indiana occurred in 1863. Southern general John Hunt Morgan led 2,500 raiders into Indiana. They captured Corydon. Several Indianans, along with some of "Morgan's Raiders," died. Indiana's soldiers fought in battles far from home. Nearly 200,000 Hoosiers served in the northern army. They helped win the war. Shortly after the war ended, President Lincoln was killed.

EDUCATION, INDUSTRIES, AND INVENTIONS

After the Civil War, Indiana college women gained some rights. Indiana University was one of the first state universities to grant women equal rights. The school graduated its first woman student in 1869.

During the late 1800s, Indiana's industries grew. Factories went up in many cities. They made glassware, cloth, farm machines, bricks, toys, band instruments, and furniture. More people moved to

Indiana. Many of them came from Europe. Between 1860 and 1900, the number of Hoosiers doubled to 2.5 million.

Indiana became a big automaking center. In 1894, Elwood Haynes of Kokomo built the first gasoline-powered car. In South Bend, the Studebaker family had made wagons and carriages since 1852. In 1902, their company began making Studebaker cars. Other Indiana-made cars included the Duesenberg, Maxwell, Auburn, and Apperson Jack Rabbit.

In 1909, a racetrack for cars opened in Indianapolis. It was named the Indianapolis Motor Speedway. Each year since 1911, a 500-mile auto

The Studebaker brothers in one of their early cars

race has been held there. Ray Harroun won the first Indianapolis 500. His average speed was 75 miles per hour. Later "Indy 500" winners have reached average speeds up to 185 miles per hour.

Northwest Indiana cities became steelmaking centers. In 1906, United States Steel Corporation founded the city of Gary. It was named for United States Steel board chairman Elbert Gary. Steel was also made in East Chicago, Hammond, and Whiting.

WORLD WARS, DEPRESSION, AND RACE RELATIONS

In 1917, the United States entered World War I (1914-1918). About 133,000 Indiana troops

Left: Ray Harroun, winner of the first Indianapolis 500, 1911
Right: Factory workers in a machine shop at Freeman Army Airfield in Seymour during World War II

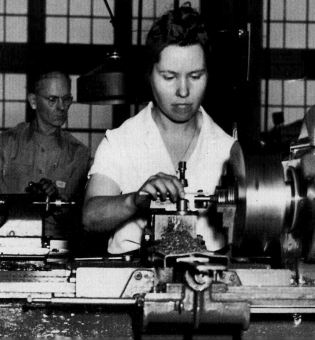

helped win the war. Hoosiers produced steel and food crops for the war effort.

Shortly after the war ended, prices for Indiana crops and factory goods fell. This helped lead to the Great Depression (1929-1939). The whole country suffered during those hard times. By 1932, Gary's steel mills were nearly shut down. One-fourth of Hoosier workers were out of work. Farmers lost their land. Indiana banks failed.

World War II (1939-1945) helped end the depression. The United States entered the war in 1941. More than 400,000 Hoosiers served in uniform. Bombs, rockets, and airplane engines made in Indiana also helped win the war. Medicines and blood plasma produced in Indiana saved thousands of wounded soldiers.

Between the two wars, Indiana's black population had doubled. But, as in other states, black Indianans were mistreated. Often, they had to attend separate schools. Then, in 1949, Indiana lawmakers made school segregation illegal. In the 1960s, blacks and whites could sit together in public places. In 1967, Richard Hatcher became the mayor of Gary. He was the first black mayor of a mid-sized American city. Hatcher was reelected four times. He worked to get more jobs and better housing in Gary.

U.S. Steel Gary works in 1914

Gary Mayor Richard Hatcher was reelected four times.

RECENT CHANGES AND PROBLEMS

Many steel mill jobs were lost during the 1980s.

Indianapolis is in Marion County. Most cities and counties have separate governments. In 1970, Indianapolis, its suburbs, and Marion County started something new. It is called Unigov. Unigov brought together city, suburban, and county government offices. Through Unigov, Indianapolis' borders include nearly all of Marion County.

Overall, Indiana has done well in the past few years. Hundreds of businesses have started in Indianapolis and other cities. They included companies from other countries. By 1993, only eight states had a lower jobless rate than Indiana.

Yet, Indiana faces problems in the 1990s. Some northwest Indiana steel mills have closed. Others have cut down on jobs. The loss of jobs has especially hurt Gary. Between 1980 and 1990, Gary lost one-fourth of its people. That is more than any other large American city lost. Many of the people who have stayed are poor. Gary is now one of America's poorest cities.

Pollution is another problem in northwest Indiana. By 1992, the steel companies had dumped tons of waste into Lake Michigan. East Chicago's Indiana Harbor is badly polluted. The United States

government has passed laws to clean up these waterways. Cleanup of Indiana Harbor should begin in 1996.

Muncie youngsters during a city cleanup campaign

Education is a statewide concern. One Hoosier in four does not even finish high school. Only one in six graduates from college. The state's lawmakers hope to change this. In 1991, Indiana spent four of every ten dollars on schools. No other state had a higher spending rate for education. Indiana is preparing young Hoosiers for the year 2000 and beyond.

Hoosiers and Their Work

HOOSIERS AND THEIR WORK

The Hoosier State has more than 5.5 million people. Only thirteen of the forty-nine other states have more people. About 90 of every 100 Hoosiers are white. Their ancestors came from such countries as England, Scotland, Ireland, and Germany. About 8 of every 100 Hoosiers are black. Only about 2 in 100 are of Spanish-speaking background. Indiana's Asian population is only 40,000. But it is growing rapidly. Today, Indiana has 13,000 American Indians.

HOOSIERS AT WORK

Nearly 3 million Hoosiers have jobs. About 625,000 of them make products. Metals are Indiana's top product. Indiana leads the country at making steel. Each year, the state makes 40 billion pounds of it. That is enough to build 20 million cars. Indiana also ranks high in making aluminum.

Transportation equipment is Indiana's second-leading product. This includes trucks and parts for cars and airplanes. The state leads the country at making musical instruments. Indiana also ranks high

Opposite: A man costumed as a voyageur (an early fur trader) during the Feast of the Hunter's Moon

A crowded beach at Indiana Dunes State Park

at making medical equipment. The state ranks third at making medicines. Indiana is also a leading producer of office furniture, glass goods, and household appliances.

More than 600,000 Hoosiers sell goods. Nearly 600,000 provide services. They include doctors, lawyers, and restaurant and gas station workers. Nearly 400,000 Hoosiers do government work. They include teachers, letter carriers, and state lawmakers.

Indiana is also a farming leader. About 100,000 Hoosiers farm. Indiana ranks fourth at growing soy-

Indiana leads the country at making steel.

beans and corn. Those are its top farm goods. The state leads the country at growing corn for popcorn. The Hoosier State is fifth at growing tomatoes. Only California produces more eggs than Indiana. Indiana is fourth at raising hogs and seventh at raising turkeys.

About 7,000 Hoosiers work in mining. Coal is Indiana's top mining product. Limestone is another important mining product. New York City's Empire State Building and many government buildings in Washington, D. C., were made of Indiana limestone. Oil, clays, and sand and gravel are also mined in the Hoosier State.

A corn harvest at the Chapman Farm, Parke County

Each year, Indiana chickens lay 5 billion eggs. That is enough for one egg for each person on earth.

Overleaf: The Bridgeton Covered Bridge, Parke County

A Hoosier State Tour

A HOOSIER STATE TOUR

*I*ndiana has big cities, small towns, and pretty countryside. It also has charming covered bridges. Places relating to early Hoosier history add to the state's charm.

THE NORTHWEST LAKESHORE

An inside view of one of Indiana's many covered bridges

Dunes are mounds of sand piled up by the wind.

Indiana's Lake Michigan shore is a good place to start a tour. Hammond lies along the lake in the state's northwest corner. Hammond has about 84,000 people. The city's Little Red Schoolhouse dates from 1869. Visitors can see the desks and books used at that time.

Just east of Hammond is Gary. It is one of the country's youngest big cities. Gary won't be 100 years old until 2006. But Gary is Indiana's fourth-biggest city. It has about 117,000 people. Gary is called the "Steel City." The United States Steel Corporation has its biggest mill there. Genesis Center opened in Gary in 1982. Circuses, rodeos, and concerts are held there.

To the east are two lakefront parks. One is Indiana Dunes State Park. The other is Indiana

Dunes National Lakeshore. Together, they cover a 22-mile strip from Gary to Michigan City. Visitors to the dunes can hike and swim.

The University of Notre Dame, with its famous golden dome

OTHER NORTHERN INDIANA HIGHLIGHTS

South Bend is in the middle of far northern Indiana. The town is on the St. Joseph River's southernmost bend. South Bend was founded in 1823. Today, it is home to almost 106,000 people. It is the state's fifth-biggest city.

The University of Notre Dame is on the northern edge of South Bend. Its Golden Dome and

Amish girls playing volleyball

An Amish blacksmith shop in Nappanee

fourteen-story library are well known. Notre Dame is also famous for football. The Fighting Irish have won the most national college football titles.

The Studebaker Museum has many old wagons, carriages, and cars. They were made by South Bend's Studebaker Company (1852-1963). A 1902 Studebaker is the museum's earliest automobile. It is an electric car.

East of South Bend is Nappanee. A 100-year-old farm called Amish Acres is there. It is a good place to learn about Amish people and their crafts. The Amish dress plainly and live simply. They refuse to fight in wars. Amish homes have no electricity. The Amish pull their plows with horses. They travel by horse and buggy. Visitors enjoy horse-drawn buggy rides at Amish Acres. They can also taste Amish foods. Shoofly pie is a famous Amish dessert. It is made with sugar and molasses.

Fort Wayne is southeast of Nappanee. Fort Wayne is Indiana's second-biggest city. It has about 173,000 people. The city grew around the fort built by General "Mad Anthony" Wayne. The old fort has been rebuilt as Historic Fort Wayne.

Johnny Appleseed Park is in Fort Wayne. Johnny's real name was John Chapman. In the early 1800s, he wandered through Indiana. He planted apple trees. Chapman died near Fort Wayne in 1845. He is buried near the park named for him. Each fall, the park hosts the Johnny Appleseed Festival.

Fort Wayne has many fine museums and a zoo. The Old City Hall Museum has information about Fort Wayne's past. The Lincoln Museum has items relating to the sixteenth president. The Telephone Museum has displays on telephone history. The Fort Wayne Children's Zoo has more than 1,000 animals. They include penguins, cheetahs, monkeys, and giraffes.

Peru is southwest of Fort Wayne. It calls itself the "Circus Capital of the World." Years ago, many circuses spent the winter there. Each summer, Peru now hosts the Circus City Festival. Young people aged seven to twenty-one perform at this circus. The International Circus Hall of Fame is in Peru. It honors famous circus performers.

Kokomo is south of Peru. The Elwood Haynes Museum is there. Visitors can see some of the first gasoline-powered cars.

Lafayette and West Lafayette are about 40 miles west of Kokomo. They stand across the Wabash River from each other. Purdue University is at West Lafayette. The school is called the "Mother of

A circus in Peru, the "Circus Capital of the World"

Astronauts." At least seventeen Purdue graduates have been chosen for space flight. Tippecanoe Battlefield and Wolf Park are other area highlights. About fifteen of the country's small number of remaining wolves live at the park. People raised these wolves at the park. Visitors can get very close to them.

INDIANAPOLIS

Indianapolis is in the middle of the state. It was founded in 1820 to be the state capital. Today, more than 730,000 people live there. No other

Left: The Soldiers and Sailors Monument, in Indianapolis Right: Marble floors and columns in the state capitol

Indiana city has even one-fourth that many people. Indianapolis is also huge in area. It covers 405 square miles. Chicago, St. Louis, Pittsburgh, and Boston could all fit inside Indianapolis.

Indianapolis is called the "Crossroads of America." This phrase is also the state motto. Interstate highways crisscross Indianapolis. The city is also a hub for trains and airplanes.

More interstate highways meet in Indiana than in any other state.

Hoosier lawmakers meet in the Indiana capitol. It is made of Indiana limestone, topped with a copper dome. Nearby is the Soldiers and Sailors Monument. This twenty-eight-story tower is also made of Indiana limestone.

The Indiana State Museum shows an 1890s Indianapolis street scene. Ice Age mammoths are also displayed. The Indianapolis Museum of Art has works from around the world. The Children's Museum of Indianapolis is the world's largest children's museum. Visitors can enter a pioneer's log cabin. They can step into an Egyptian mummy's tomb. The museum also has the world's biggest model train collection.

The Children's Museum of Indianapolis

The Benjamin Harrison Home is open to visitors. Harrison was the twenty-third president of the United States (1889-1893). Before and after he was president, Harrison lived in Indianapolis. William

Indianapolis Motor Speedway Hall of Fame Museum

A costumed woman demonstrates baking in a Conner Prairie kitchen.

Henry Harrison was his grandfather. The sixteen-room home has Benjamin's furniture and paintings. Dolls that belonged to his children are displayed there, too.

Indianapolis is also a sports center. The Indianapolis Colts play football there. The Indiana Pacers play pro basketball. The state high-school basketball tournament is held in March. The movie *Hoosiers* is about this popular tournament. Each Memorial Day weekend, the city hosts the "Indy 500" auto race.

OTHER CENTRAL INDIANA HIGHLIGHTS

Noblesville is just north of Indianapolis. Conner Prairie is there. It is a restored 1830s village. Costumed guides show how the pioneers made pottery and furniture. A blacksmith shows how horseshoes were made.

Muncie is northeast of Indianapolis. Ball State University is there. The school's name honors the Ball family. Their Muncie company made the famous Ball jars. People preserved food in those jars.

New Castle is south of Muncie. The Indiana Basketball Hall of Fame is there. Visitors learn what basketball means to Hoosiers. Fountain City is to the east. The Levi Coffin House still stands there. Levi and Katie Coffin hid hundreds of slaves in their home. A secret room served as a hiding place.

Columbus is south of Indianapolis. The city is called the "Architectural Showplace of America." In 1942, the North Christian Church was completed. Eero Saarinen had designed it. Other great architects also designed buildings for Columbus. John M. Johansen created the Smith Elementary School. It is made up of many small buildings. They are connected by colorful, tube-shaped ramps. Columbus now has more than fifty buildings designed by famous architects.

Two of the many buildings that helped give Columbus the name "Architectural Showplace of America" are the Cummins Engine Company (left) and the North Christian Church (right).

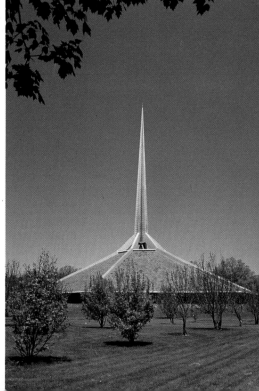

Nashville is west of Columbus. The Brown County Art Colony began there about 100 years ago. Visitors enjoy Nashville's craft shops and art galleries.

Indiana University is west of Nashville at Bloomington. The school's Lilly Library has thousands of rare works. They include an original copy of the Declaration of Independence.

Terre Haute is northwest of Bloomington. The city's name is French for "high land." The Paul Dresser Birthplace is in Terre Haute. Dresser wrote the state song, "On the Banks of the Wabash, Far Away." The river can be seen from his home. Indiana State University (ISU) is also in Terre

Haute. ISU's Hook Observatory has a big telescope. With it, visitors can see the stars and planets.

North of Terre Haute is Parke County. The county has more than thirty covered bridges. No other county in the country has as many. Some are almost 150 years old. The Parke County Covered Bridge Festival is held each fall.

SOUTHERN INDIANA

Vincennes is Indiana's oldest town. The French founded the town in 1732. It lies on the Wabash River in southwestern Indiana. Today, visitors can tour the George Rogers Clark Memorial. It honors Clark's work during the Revolutionary War. The Indiana Territory's capitol is also open to visitors. There, they can see a model of Indiana's first print shop. Grouseland was territorial governor William Henry Harrison's home. It was Indiana's first brick building.

Evansville is due south of Vincennes. It is on the Ohio River. Mound-building Indians had a village there about 1250. Eleven mounds still stand. They are part of Angel Mounds Memorial. Buildings from the village have been reconstructed. Pioneers first settled in Evansville in 1812. Today,

The George Rogers Clark Memorial, at Vincennes

43

the city has more than 126,000 people. It is Indiana's third-biggest city. Visitors enjoy the Evansville Museum of Arts and Science. Its Rivertown USA shows a river village of 100 years ago. The museum also has great paintings.

Northeast of Evansville is Lincoln City. Outside that town is the farm where Abraham Lincoln grew up (1816-1830). It is now the Lincoln Boyhood National Memorial. Visitors can walk the trails that Lincoln walked. They can also enter a log cabin. It is like the one in which Lincoln lived.

Just east of Lincoln's home is Santa Claus. This town was named at Christmastime in 1846. In 1946, Holiday World was built. It was the country's first theme park. The park has rides and toy and doll museums. Visitors can meet Santa and his helpers.

Wyandotte Cave is north of Santa Claus. It is one of North America's largest caves. Monument Mountain is inside the cave. The mountain stands 135 feet high. It is the world's largest underground mountain.

Corydon is east of Wyandotte Cave. The town was Indiana's first state capital. The blue limestone capitol looks like it did in 1816. Governor Hendricks's Home is near the capitol. It shows Indiana homelife between 1820 and 1880.

Farther east is Jeffersonville. It is on the Ohio River. The Hillerich & Bradsby Company is there. It makes the famous Louisville Slugger baseball bats. They were named for Louisville, Kentucky. That city is across the Ohio River from Jeffersonville. Visitors can tour the plant and see the bats being made.

North along the Ohio River is Rising Sun. It is a good place to end an Indiana tour. The town was settled in 1798. The settlers named it for the beautiful sunrises over the Ohio River. Many buildings from the 1800s are preserved at Rising Sun. A good way to see them is by riding the Rising Sun Trolley.

A bronzed cabin fireplace at the Lincoln Boyhood National Memorial

Rising Sun is across the Ohio River from Rabbit Hash, Kentucky.

45

A Gallery of Famous Hoosiers

Many Hoosiers have become famous. They include basketball stars, authors, astronauts, and presidents.

Frances Slocum (1773-1847) lived in Pennsylvania. When she was five years old, Delaware Indians kidnapped her. She lived with Indians the rest of her life. Sometime after 1794, she married a Miami Indian chief. They settled near present-day Peru, Indiana. In 1837, her brothers and sisters found her. But she refused to leave her Indian family. Frances Slocum State Forest near Peru is named for her.

Sarah Breedlove Walker (1867-1919) was born in Louisiana. In 1910, she moved to Indianapolis. Sarah was known as "Madame C. J. Walker." She founded a company. It made hair products for black women. She became the first black woman millionaire. Walker helped many charities. After she died, the Madame Walker Urban Life Center was built. Plays and concerts are held there.

The Hoosier State has produced many fine authors. **Lew Wallace** (1827-1905) was born in Brookville. He is best known for his novel *Ben Hur*

Opposite: Poet James Whitcomb Riley, surrounded by children

Lew Wallace (below) was the son of Indiana governor David Wallace.

(1880). It is about early Christians in the Roman Empire. Before that, Wallace had been a Civil War general. A statue of him is in the U.S. Capitol in Washington, D. C.

James Whitcomb Riley (1849-1916) was born in Greenfield. He won fame as "The Hoosier Poet." Children loved his poems. "The Old Swimmin' Hole" and "Little Orphant Annie" were favorites.

Riley's "Little Orphant Annie" inspired the comic strip character "Little Orphan Annie."

Gene Stratton Porter (1868-1924) was born near Wabash. She lived on the edge of the Limberlost. This was an Indiana swamp. Porter studied the plants and animals there. Later, she wrote about these things. Movies were made from her novels *Laddie* and *Girl of the Limberlost*.

Booth Tarkington (1869-1946) was born in Indianapolis. *The Gentlemen from Indiana* (1889) started him on the road as a writer. *Penrod* and *Seventeen* are among his works for young people.

Theodore Dreiser

Theodore Dreiser (1871-1945) was born in Terre Haute. He wrote about the unpleasant sides of American life. His novels include *Sister Carrie* and *An American Tragedy*. **Paul Dresser** (1857-1906) was Dreiser's older brother. Paul changed the spelling of his last name. He wrote "On the Banks of the Wabash, Far Away" in 1899. Later, it became Indiana's state song.

Jessamyn West (1902-1984) was born in southern Indiana's Jennings County. She was raised as a Quaker. Her best-known book is *The Friendly Persuasion*. It is about an Indiana Quaker family during the Civil War.

Kurt Vonnegut, Jr., was born in Indianapolis in 1922. Vonnegut became a soldier and was captured in World War II. Later, he wrote stories about war and human cruelty. *Cat's Cradle* and *Slaughterhouse Five* are among his works. Ernie Pyle (1900-1945) was born on a farm near Dana. He became a newspaper reporter. During World War II, Pyle wrote first-hand reports from battlefields. His

Left: Booth Tarkington
Right: Jessamyn West

Cole Porter

work won a 1944 Pulitzer Prize. In 1945, he was killed during the Okinawa campaign.

Jim Davis was born in Marion in 1945. He became a cartoonist. In 1978, he started drawing the "Garfield" comic strip. Those cartoons have been reprinted in many books. They have sold more than 60 million copies.

Two great songwriters were Hoosiers. **Cole Porter** (1891-1964) was born in Peru. He wrote "Night and Day" and "Begin the Beguine." **Hoagy Carmichael** (1899-1981) was a Bloomington native. Carmichael's best-known song is "Stardust." He also wrote "Georgia on My Mind." That is now Georgia's state song.

Some popular entertainers have been Hoosiers. **Richard "Red" Skelton** was born in Vincennes in 1913. At first, Skelton worked as a circus clown. Later, he became a famous comedian on radio and television. **James Dean** (1931-1955) was born in Marion. He became a great actor. *Rebel Without a Cause* is one of his best-known movies. He was only twenty-four when he died in a car crash. **David Letterman** was born in Indianapolis in 1947. For a while, he worked as a television weatherman in Indianapolis. Letterman later became a famous comedian and talk-show host.

Twyla Tharp was born in Portland, Indiana, in 1941. She became a dancer and choreographer. Her jazz ballets include *The Raggedy Dances*. She also created dances for *Hair* and other movies.

Michael Jackson was born in Gary in 1958. In the 1960s and 1970s, he was the star of the Jackson Five. In 1978, he started singing on his own. His album *Thriller* (1982) has sold over 40 million copies. That is more than any other album.

Orville Redenbacher was born in Brazil, Indiana, in 1907. In his youth, he grew corn that could be made into popcorn. Orville Redenbacher's popcorn is now sold throughout the country. He is called the "King of Popcorn."

Choreographers plan the steps and movements in ballets and musicals.

Left: Twyla Tharp
Right: James Dean

Larry Bird

Gus Grissom and two other astronauts died in a fire while testing the first three-man spacecraft.

Mordecai "Three Finger" Brown (1876-1948) was born in Nyesville. When he was seven, he caught his hand in a farm machine. One finger was lost. Another could no longer be used. Yet, "Three Finger" Brown became a great pitcher. He was elected to the Baseball Hall of Fame.

Basketball greats **Oscar "The Big O" Robertson** and **Larry Bird** were Hoosiers. Robertson was born in Tennessee in 1938. However, he grew up in Indianapolis. There, he went to Crispus Attucks High School. Robertson led the school to two straight state basketball titles. Later, he played pro basketball for fourteen years. "The Big O" scored 26,710 points in those years. Bird was born in French Lick in 1956. He starred at Indiana State University. Later, he led the Boston Celtics to three championships (1981, 1984, and 1986).

Three Hoosiers helped us understand space. **Harold Urey** (1893-1981) was born in Walkerton. He studied what the sun and planets were made of. Urey won the 1934 Nobel Prize in chemistry. Astronaut **Virgil "Gus" Grissom** (1926-1967) was born in Mitchell. In 1965, he took part in the country's first two-person space flight. Astronaut **Frank Borman** was born in Gary in 1928. He command-

ed the 1968 *Apollo 8* mission. It was the first *Harold Urey*
manned flight to orbit the moon.

The birthplace of Gus Grissom, Jessamyn West,
Larry Bird, and "Three Finger" Brown . . .
Home also to Frances Slocum, Madame C. J.
Walker, Abraham Lincoln, and Benjamin Harrison . . .
Site of the Indianapolis 500, Lincoln's Boyhood
Home, Wyandotte Cave, and a town called Santa
Claus . . .
A state that provides the country with steel,
coal, and corn for popping. . .
This is Indiana—the Hoosier State.

Did You Know?

Albert Von Tilzer of Indianapolis wrote the song "Take Me Out to the Ball Game."

In 1914, *Indianapolis Star* cartoonist John Gruelle began making up stories about his daughter's doll. The doll was called Raggedy Ann from a character in a James Whitcomb Riley poem. Gruelle then began writing books about Raggedy Ann. The doll became a popular children's toy.

Some people string popcorn for holiday decorations. Indiana grew a record 150 million pounds of corn for popping in 1981. That was enough to make a popcorn string 3 million miles long, or thirteen times the distance between the earth and the moon.

Indiana has towns named Beanblossom, Gnaw Bone, Correct, Jockey, Carefree, Daylight, Hoosierville, Chili, and Popcorn. The state's many towns with the same names as countries include Brazil, China, Cuba, Denmark, Ireland, Lebanon, Mexico, Norway, Peru, and Poland.

Richard Arvin of Indianapolis invented the car heater in the 1920s.

Indiana has produced five vice presidents of the United States. They were Schuyler Colfax (1869-1873), Thomas Hendricks (1885), Charles Fairbanks (1905-1909), Thomas Marshall (1913-1921), and Dan Quayle (1989-1993).

John Powell created the first mechanical corn picker at Kokomo in the 1920s.

A Kokomo-area man set a hot-air balloon record in 1934. William Kepner rose 11.5 miles high. The balloon fell apart, and Kepner parachuted to safety when he was only 300 feet from the ground.

In 1870, the country's first college sorority started at DePauw University in Greencastle, Indiana. This group for college women is still called Kappa Alpha Theta.

The southern Indiana town of English flooded in 1990. English's business district was then moved 2 miles northeast to higher ground.

Sideburns were named after Ambrose Burnside. This Liberty native became a Civil War general. He grew a very bushy beard on the sides of his cheeks. These side-whiskers became known as sideburns.

In 1990, Shakamak High School students made the world's biggest yo-yo. It weighed 820 pounds. When it was launched from a 160-foot crane, it "yo-yoed" twelve times. Students at the same Indiana high school made the world's biggest–and perhaps the loudest–guitar in 1991. The guitar weighs 1,865 pounds and stands 38 feet tall.

INDIANA INFORMATION

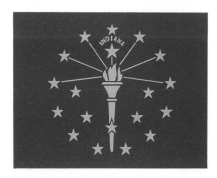

State flag

Peony

Cardinal

Area: 36,291 square miles (only twelve states are smaller)

Greatest Distance North to South: 275 miles

Greatest Distance East to West: 160 miles

Borders: Michigan and Lake Michigan to the north; Ohio to the east; Kentucky to the south and southeast; Illinois to the west

Highest Point: 1,257 feet above sea level, near Richmond

Lowest Point: 320 feet above sea level, along the Ohio River in Posey County

Hottest Recorded Temperature: 116° F. (at Collegeville, on July 14, 1936)

Coldest Recorded Temperature: -36° F. (at New Whiteland, on January 19, 1994)

Statehood: The nineteenth state, on December 11, 1816

Origin of Name: *Indiana* was named for the American Indians and means "land of the Indians"

Capital: Indianapolis (since 1825)

Previous Capitals: Vincennes (1800-1813) and Corydon (1813-1825)

Counties: 92

United States Representatives: 10 (as of 1992)

State Senators: 50

State Representatives: 100

State Song: "On the Banks of the Wabash, Far Away," by Paul Dresser

State Motto: "The Crossroads of America"

Nickname: "The Hoosier State"

State Seal: Adopted in 1963

State Flag: Adopted in 1917

State Flower: Peony

State Bird: Cardinal

State Tree: Tulip tree

State Stone: Indiana limestone

State Poem: "Indiana," by Arthur Franklin Mapes

Some Rivers: Wabash, Tippecanoe, Eel, Kankakee, White, Ohio, Maumee, St. Marys, and two named St. Joseph (one flows through South Bend; the other is northeast of Fort Wayne)

Lakes: Wawasee, Manitou, Maxinkuckee, Turkey, Monroe, Mississinewa

Wildlife: Deer, foxes, beavers, raccoons, opossums, squirrels, cardinals, bluebirds, sparrows, robins, woodpeckers, wrens, ducks, blue herons, eagle, horned owls, quails, many other kinds of birds, catfish, bass, salmon, bluegills, many other kinds of fish

Manufactured Products: Steel and aluminum, auto parts, aircraft parts, other transportation equipment, telephone and television equipment, other electrical equipment, medicines and other chemicals, office furniture, glass goods, medical equipment, musical instruments, baked goods, dairy products, soft drinks, hardwood lumber, rubber goods, plastic goods, plumbing and heating equipment

Farm Products: Corn, soybeans, oats, wheat, alfalfa, hay, tomatoes, snap beans, cucumbers, watermelons, apples, eggs, chickens, hogs, turkeys, milk

Mining Products: Coal, limestone, oil, cement, clays, crushed stone, sand and gravel

Population: 5,544,159, fourteenth among the states (1990 U. S. Census Bureau figures)

Major Cities (1990 Census):

Indianapolis	731,327	Hammond	84,236
Fort Wayne	173,072	Muncie	71,035
Evansville	126,272	Bloomington	60,633
Gary	116,646	Anderson	59,459
South Bend	105,511	Terre Haute	57,483

Tulip tree

Tulip tree leaves and blossom

INDIANA HISTORY

8000 B.C.—Prehistoric Indians reach Indiana

1679—French explorer La Salle reaches present-day South Bend

1681—La Salle meets with Miami Indians under the "Council Oak" in South Bend

1732—The French begin building a fort near present-day Vincennes

1754-1763—England wins the French and Indian War between England and France and gains Indiana and other lands from France

1775—The Americans begin the Revolutionary War

1779—George Rogers Clark's forces capture Vincennes

1783—The peace treaty ending the Revolutionary War is signed; England's lands east of the Mississippi, including Indiana, become part of the United States

1787—The U.S. Congress creates the Northwest Territory, which includes Indiana

1790—Miami chief Little Turtle's warriors defeat U.S. soldiers near present-day Fort Wayne

1794—General "Mad Anthony" Wayne defeats the Miami Indians in the Battle of Fallen Timbers

1800—Indiana, with 5,641 people, becomes a separate territory

1811—William Henry Harrison defeats the Indians in the Battle of Tippecanoe

1816—On December 11, Indiana becomes the nineteenth state

1825—Indianapolis becomes the permanent state capital; Indiana Seminary (now Indiana University) opens at Bloomington; Robert Owen purchases New Harmony

1826-47—Levi and Katie Coffin live in Fountain City, where they help over 2,000 slaves reach freedom

1841—William Henry Harrison becomes the ninth president of the United States, but dies after only one month in office

1842—The University of Notre Dame is founded

1861—Abraham Lincoln becomes the sixteenth president of the United States; the Civil War begins

1865—The North wins the Civil War; President Lincoln is assassinated

1869—Purdue University is founded

1888—Indiana's present state capitol is completed

1894—Elwood Haynes of Kokomo builds one of the world's first gasoline-powered automobiles

1902—The Studebaker Company begins making automobiles in South Bend

1906—Gary is founded as a steelmaking city

1911—The first Indianapolis 500 auto race is held

1917-18—After the United States enters World War I, about 133,000 Hoosiers serve

1929-39—Indiana steelmaking, coal mining, farming, and banking suffer during the Great Depression

1941-45—After the United States enters World War II, over 400,000 Hoosiers serve

1949—Indiana makes segregation illegal in public schools

1967—Richard Hatcher is elected as one of the first black mayors of a mid-sized U.S. city

1970—The Port of Indiana at Burns Harbor opens to serve oceangoing ships; the Unigov program unites the governments of Indianapolis and Marion County

1974—A series of tornadoes kills more than fifty Hoosiers

1982—Katie Hall becomes the first black member of the U.S. House of Representatives from Indiana

1990—The Hoosier State's population is 5,544,159

An 1894 picture of Elwood Haynes in his gasoline-powered automobile

MAP KEY

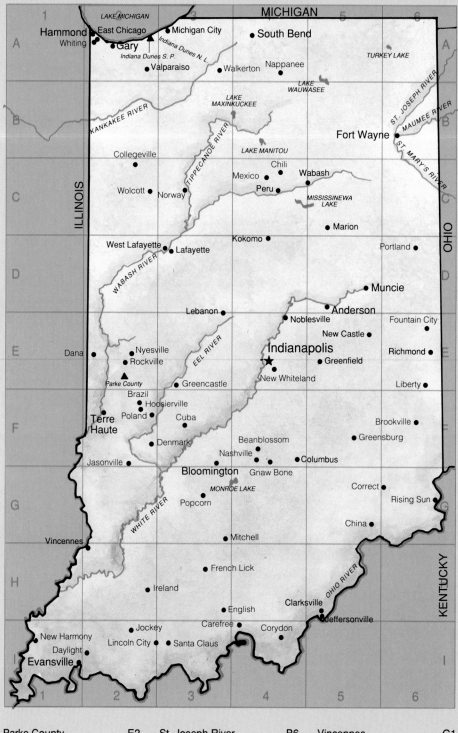

Anderson	D5
Beanblossom	F4
Bloomington	G3
Brazil	F2
Brookville	F6
Carefree	I4
Chili	C4
China	G5
Clarksville	H5
Collegeville	C2
Columbus	F4
Correct	G5
Corydon	I4
Cuba	F3
Dana	E2
Daylight	I2
Denmark	F2
East Chicago	A2
Eel River	E3
English	H3
Evansville	I1
Fort Wayne	B6
Fountain City	E6
French Lick	H3
Gary	A2
Gnaw Bone	G4
Greencastle	E3
Greenfield	E5
Greensburg	F5
Hammond	A2
Hoosierville	F2
Indiana Dunes National Lakeshore	A3
Indiana Dunes State Park	A2
Indianapolis	E4
Ireland	H2
Jasonville	F2
Jeffersonville	H5
Jockey	I2
Kankakee River	B2
Kokomo	D4
Lafayette	D3
Lake Michigan	D2
Lake Manitou	B4
Lake Maxinkuckee	B4
Lake Wauwasee	B5
Lebanon	D3
Liberty	E6
Lincoln City	I2
Marion	C5
Maumee River	B6
Mexico	C4
Michigan City	A3
Mississinewa Lake	C5
Mitchell	G3
Monroe Lake	G4
Muncie	D5
Nappanee	A4
Nashville	F4
New Castle	E5
New Harmony	I1
New Whiteland	E4
Noblesville	E4
Norway	C3
Nyesville	E2
Ohio River	H5

Parke County	E2
Peru	C4
Poland	F2
Popcorn	G3
Portland	D6
Richmond	E6
Rising Sun	G6
Rockville	E2

St. Joseph River	B6
St. Mary's River	B,C6
Santa Claus	I3
South Bend	A4
Terre Haute	F2
Tippecanoe River	B,C3
Turkey Lake	A6
Valparaiso	A2

Vincennes	G1
Wabash	C4
Wabash River	D2
Walkerton	A3
West Lafayette	D2
White River	G2
Whiting	A2
Wolcott	C2

GLOSSARY

ancestor: A relative who lived long ago, such as a great-grandmother or a great-great-grandfather

ancient: Relating to a time early in history

architect: A person who draws the plans for buildings

astronaut: A person who is highly trained for spaceflight

capital: The city that is the seat of government

capitol: The building in which the government meets

choreographer: A person who arranges and directs the steps and movements in a ballet or musical

constitution: A framework of government or set of basic laws

dune: A mound of sand that was piled up by the wind

explorer: A person who visits and studies unknown lands

mammoths and mastodons: Prehistoric animals in the elephant family

manufacturing: The making of products

million: A thousand thousand (1,000,000)

pioneer: A person who is among the first to move into a region

pollution: The harming or dirtying of the environment

population: The number of people in a place

prehistoric: Belonging to the time before written history

segregation: The process of keeping people apart because of race or other reasons

slavery: A practice in which people are owned by other people

territory: Land owned by a country; a part of the United States that is not a state but that has a government

tornado: A funnel-shaped windstorm that causes great damage when it touches land

transportation: The process of moving things

A steam tractor, Parke County

PICTURE ACKNOWLEDGMENTS

Front cover, © Gene Ahrens/**SuperStock**; 1, © J. Madeley/**Root Resources**; 2, **Tom Dunnington**; 3, © Cheryl A. Ertelt/ **N E Stock Photo**; 5, **Tom Dunnington**; 6-7, © **Tom Till**; 8, © Peter Pearson/**Tony Stone Images, Inc.**; 9 (left), © Michael Shedlock/**N E Stock Photo**; 9 (right), **Courtesy Hammond, Incorporated, Maplewood, New Jersey**; 10 (top), © John Mielcarek/**Dembinsky Photo Assoc.**; 10 (bottom left), © **James P. Rowan**; 10 (bottom right), © Michael Shedlock/**N E Stock Photo**; 11, © **Tom Till**; 12, © **James P. Rowan**; 13, © **James P. Rowan**; 15, © Michael Shedlock/ **N E Stock Photo**; 16 (top), © **James P. Rowan/Tony Stone Images, Inc.**; 16 (bottom), © **James P. Rowan**; 17 (top), **North Wind Picture Archives**; 17 (bottom), © **James P. Rowan**; 18, **Stock Montage, Inc.**; 19, © **Ruth Chin**; 20, © W. J. Scott/**H. Armstrong Roberts**; 21, © Michael Shedlock/**N E Stock Photo**; 22, **Courtesy Fulton County Historical Society, Inc.**; 23, **Indiana State Archives**; 24 (left), **Photo courtesy Indianapolis Motor Speedway**; 24 (right), **Indiana State Archives**; 25 (top), **U. S. Steel, Inc.**; 25 (bottom), **A/P Wide World Photos**; 26, © J. H. Boulet, Jr./**Root Resources**; 27, © **Cameramann International, Ltd.**; 28, © James P. Rowan/**Tony Stone Images, Inc.**; 29, © **James P. Rowan**; 30, © **Cameramann International, Ltd.**; 31, © Michael Shedlock/**N E Stock Photo**; 32-33, © Michael Shedlock/**N E Stock Photo**; 34, © Gail Nachel/**Root Resources**; 35, © William Strode/**SuperStock**; 36 (top), © D. & I. MacDonald/**Root Resources**; 36 (bottom), © Michael Shedlock/**N E Stock Photo**; 37, © **Ruth Chin**; 38 (left), © Cathlyn Melloan/**Tony Stone Images, Inc.**; 38 (right), © M. Gibson/**H. Armstrong Roberts**; 39, © **Joan Dunlop**; 40 (top), © **P. Michael Whye**; 40 (bottom), © **Joan Dunlop**; 41 (both pictures), © Cathlyn Melloan/**Tony Stone Images, Inc.**; 42, © **Lani**/**Photri**; 43, © Tom Dietrich/**Tony Stone Images, Inc.**; 45, © **Tom Till**; 46, **AP/Wide World Photos**; 47, **Indiana State Archives**; 48, **AP/Wide World Photos**; 49 (left), **North Wind Picture Archives**; 49 (right), **AP/Wide World Photos**; 50, **AP/Wide World Photos**; 51 (both pictures), **AP/Wide World Photos**; 52, **AP/Wide World Photos**; 53, **AP/Wide World Photos**; 54 (bottom), **Hasbro, Inc.**; 54 (top), **Photo courtesy of the Popcorn Institute**; 55 (top), **The Children's Museum of Indianapolis**; 55 (bottom), **DePauw University Archives and Special Collections**; 56 (top), **Courtesy Flag Research Center, Winchester, Massachusetts 01890**; 56 (middle), © Mary Kay Desotelle/**mga/Photri**; 56 (bottom), © John Mielcarek/**Dembinsky Photo Assoc.**; 57 (top), © Kitty Kohout/**Root Resources**; 57 (bottom), © **Ruth Chin**; 59, **Stock Montage, Inc.**; 60, **Tom Dunnington**; 62, © **Tom Till**; back cover, © **Tom Till**

INDEX

Page numbers in boldface type indicate illustrations.

American Indians (Native Americans), 4, 13-14, 29, 43
Amish, 36, **36**
Amish Acres, 36
Anderson, 57
Angel Mounds Memorial, 43
Angel Mounds State Park, 13
architecture, 41, **41**
astronauts, 52-53
automaking, 23, **23**, 36, 59, **59**
Ball State University, 40
Bird, Larry, 4, 52
birds, 10, **10**
Bloomington, 42, 50, 57, 58
Borman, Frank, 52-53
Brazil (town), 51, 54
Bridgeton Covered Bridge, **32-33**
Brookville, 47
Brown, Mordecai, 52
Brown County Art Colony, 42
Burns Harbor, 59
Burnside, Ambrose, 55
capital. *See* Corydon; Indianapolis; Vincennes
Carmichael, Hoagy, 50
Cataract Falls State Park, **11, back cover**
Chapman, John, 36-37
Chellberg Farm, **15**
Children's Museum, 39, **39**
Civil War, 21-22, **22**, 55, 59
Clark, George Rogers, 15-16, **16**, 58
memorial of, 43, **43**
climate, 10-11, 56
coal, 4, 20
Coffin, Katie and Levi, 21, 41, 58
Colfax, Schuyler, 54
Collegeville, 56
Columbus, 41, **41**
Conner Prairie, 40, **40**
constitution, 20
Corydon, 19, **19**, 22, 44, 56
Council Oak, 14, 58
covered bridges, **32-33, 34**, 43, **back cover**

Cowles Bog, **10**
Davis, Jim, 50
Dean, James, 50, **51**
Delaware Indians, 14, 47
DePaul University, 55
Dreiser, Theodore, 48, **48**
Dresser, Paul, 48
birthplace of, 42
East Chicago, 24, 26
education, 20-21, 25, 27, 59
Eel River, 57
elevation, 56
employment, 26, 29-31
ethnic people, 29
Evansville, 43-44, 57
Fairbanks, Charles, 54
Fallen Timbers, battle of, 58
farming, 4, 30-31, **31, 54, 57, 62**
Feast of the Hunter's Moon, 1, **2, 28**
fish, 10
forests, 9-10, **10, 57, back cover**
Fort Wayne, 17, **17**, 36-37, 57, 58
Fort Wayne River, 57
Fountain City, 21, 41, 58
French and Indian War, 15, 58
French Lick, 52
Gary, 24, 25, 26, 34, 35, 51, 52, 57, 59
Gary, Elbert, 24
Genesis Center, 34
Great Depression, 25, 59
Great Lakes, 8
Greencastle, 55
Grissom, Virgil, 52
Grouseland, 43
Gruelle, John, 54
Hall, Katie, 59
Hammond, 24, 34, 57
Harrison, Benjamin, 39
Harrison, William Henry, 17, **17**, 39-40, 43, 58
Harroun, Ray, 24, **24**
Hatcher, Richard, 25, **25**, 59
Haynes, Elwood, 23, 59, **59**
Museum of, 37

Hendricks, Thomas, 54
home of, 44
highways, 39
Historic Fort Wayne, 36
history, 13-27, 58-59
Holiday World, 44
Hook Observatory, 43
Hoosier, Sam, 20
Illinois, 8, 16, 17, 19, 56
Indiana Basketball Hall of Fame, 40
Indiana Dunes, **6-7, 8,15, 29**, 34-35
Indiana Harbor, 26, 27
Indianapolis, 19, 23, 26, 38-40, **38, 39, 40**, 48, 50, 52, 56, 57, 58, 59, **front cover**
Indianapolis 500, 4, 23-24, **24**, 40, **40**, 59
Indianapolis Museum of Art, 39
Indiana Seminary, 58
Indiana State Museum, 39
Indiana State University, 42-43, 52
Indiana University, 22, **42**, 42, 58
industries, 22-24, 29-30, **30, 57**
International Circus Hall of Fame, 37
Jackson, Michael, 51
Jeffersonville, 45
Johansen, John M., 41
Johnny Appleseed Festival, 37
Johnny Appleseed Park, 36
Kankakee River, 9, 57
Kentucky, 8, 56
Kepner, William, 55
Kickapoo Indians, 14
Kokomo, 37, 54, 55, 59
Lafayette, 14, 37
Lake Michigan, 8, 26, 34, 56
lakes, 8, 57
La Salle, René-Robert Cavelier, Sieur de, 14, 58
Letterman, David, 50
Limberlost, 48
limestone, 31, 39, 57
Lincoln, Abraham, 18-19, 22, 44, 59
Boyhood National Memorial, 44, **45**

Lincoln City, 44
Lincoln Museum, 37
literature, 47-50
Little Red Schoolhouse, 34
Little Turtle, 16-17, 58
Manitou Lake, 57
Mapes, Arthur Franklin, 57
maps of Indiana showing:
  cities and geographical features, **60**
  location in U.S., **2**
  products and history, **5**
  topography, **9**
Marion County, 26, 50, 59
Marshall, Thomas, 54
Maumee River, 57
Maxinkuckee Lake, 57
Miami Indians, 13-14, 16, 47, 58
Michigan, 8, 17, 56
Michigan City, **1**, 35
mining, 4, 31, 57
Mississinewa Lake, 57
Mississippi River, 16
Mitchell, 52
Monroe Lake, 57
Monument Mountain, 44
Morgan, John Hunt, 22
Muncie, 40, 57
Nappanee, 36
Nashville, 42
New Castle, 40-41
New Harmony, **20**, 21, **21**, 58
New Whiteland, 56
nicknames, 4, 20, 56
Noblesville, 40
North Christian Church, 41, **41**
Northwest Territory, 16, 58
Notre Dame, University of, **3**, 4,
  35-36, **35**, 59
Nyesville, 52
Ohio, 8, 56

Ohio River, 9, 43, 45, 56, 57
Old City Hall Museum, 37
Owen, Robert, 21, 58
Parke County, 43, **62**
Peru (town), 37, **37**, 47, 50, 54
plants, **9**, 10, **10**
pollution, 26-27, **27**
population, 19, 23, 57, 58, 59
Porter, Cole, 50, **50**
Porter, Gene Stratton, 48
Portland, 51
Port of Indiana, 59
Posey County, 56
Powell, John, 54
Purdue University, 4, 37-38, 59
Pyle, Ernie, 49-50
Quayle, Dan, 54
Raggedy Ann, 54, **54**
Rapp, George, 21
Redenbacher, Orville, 51
Revolutionary War, 15-16, 43, 58
Richmond, 56
Riley, James Whitcomb, **47**, 48, 54
Rising Sun, 45
rivers, 8-9, 11, 57
Rivertown USA, 44
Robertson, Oscar "The Big O," 52
Saarinen, Eero, 41
St. Joseph River, 35, 57
St. Marys River, 57
Santa Claus (town), 4, 44
Shawnee Indians, 14, 17-18
Skelton, Richard (Red), 50
slavery, 16, 21, 22
Slocum, Frances, 47
Soldiers and Sailors Monument, **38**, 39
South Bend, 14, 23, 35-36, 57, 58, 59
South Bend River, 57
sports, 40, 52
square miles, 8, 56

state capitol, **19**, **38**, 59, **front cover**
statehood, 19, 56, 58
state symbols, 9, 10, 48, 56-57, **56-57**
steelmaking, 4, 24, **25**, 26, 29, **30**, 34,
  59
Studebaker Museum, 36
Tarkington, Booth, 48, **49**
Tecumseh, 17-18
Telephone Museum, 37
Tenskwatawa, 17-18
Terre Haute, 42-43, 48, 57
Tharp, Twyla, 4, 51, **51**
Tilzer, Albert Von, 54
Tippecanoe, Battle of, **18**, 38, 58
Tippecanoe River, 9, 57
topography, 8-9, **9**
Turkey Lake, 57
Underground Railroad, 21, 41, 58
Unigov, 26, 59
Urey, Harold, 52, **53**
Vincennes, 14, 16, 17, 43, **43**, 50, 56,
  58
Vonnegut, Kurt, Jr., 49
Wabash River, 8-9, 37, 43, 57
Walker, Sarah Breedlove, 47
Walkerton, 52
Wallace, Lew, 47-48, **47**
Wawasee Lake, 8, 57
Wayne, "Mad Anthony," 16-17, 36,
  58
West, Jessamyn, 49, **49**
West Lafayette, 37
White River, 9, 57
Whiting, 24
wildlife, 10, **10**, 57
Wisconsin, 17
Wolf Park, 38
World War I, 24-25, 59
World War II, **24**, 25, 59
Wyandotte Cave, 44

ABOUT THE AUTHORS

Dennis and Judith Fradin have coauthored several books in the From Sea to Shining Sea series. The Fradins both graduated from Northwestern University in 1967. Dennis has been a professional writer for twenty years, and has published 150 books. His works for Childrens Press include the Young People's Stories of Our States series, the Disaster! series, and the Thirteen Colonies series. Judith earned her M.A. in literature from Northwestern University and taught high-school and college English for many years. The Fradins, who are the parents of Anthony, Diana, and Michael, live in Evanston, Illinois.